American Moments

ABDO
Daughters

THE BATTLE
OF THE ALAMO

By Cory Gunderson

VISIT US AT
WWW.ABDOPUB.COM

Published by ABDO Publishing Company, 4940 Viking Drive, Suite 622, Edina, Minnesota 55435. Copyright ©2004 by Abdo Consulting Group, Inc. International copyrights reserved in all countries. No part of this book may be reproduced in any form without written permission from the publisher.

Printed in the United States.

Edited by: Sheila Rivera
Contributing Editor: Kate A. Conley
Interior Production and Design: Terry Dunham Incorporated
Cover Design: Mighty Media
Photos: Corbis, Library of Congress, Wildside Press

Library of Congress Cataloging-in-Publication Data

Gunderson, Cory Gideon.
   The battle of the Alamo / Cory Gunderson.
      p. cm. -- (American moments)
   Includes index.
   Summary: An overview of the history of the struggle between the Texas settlers and Mexico's General Santa Anna for control of Texas, with a detailed description of the 1836 siege of the Alamo.
   Contents: Early Texas history -- Military strife -- Battle of the Alamo -- Republic of Texas -- Annexation -- Remember the Alamo.
   ISBN 1-59197-278-7
   1. Alamo (San Antonio, Tex.)--Siege, 1836--Juvenile literature. [1. Alamo (San Antonio, Tex.)--Siege, 1836. 2. Texas--History--To 1846.] I. Title. II. Series.

F390.G88 2003
976.4'03--dc21
                                                                              .
                                                              2003044339

CONTENTS

THE ALAMO

The Alamo in San Antonio, Texas, is one of the most famous historical landmarks in the United States. This monument stands as a reminder of the battle for independence fought there in 1836. Some have called the Alamo the shrine of Texas liberty.

There is more to the story of the Alamo than just one battle, however. The Alamo was originally a mission built by the Catholic Church. It was named the Mission San Antonio de Valero. Established in 1718, it was one of five Spanish missions created by the Franciscans. All of these missions were built in present-day San Antonio. Their purpose was to convert the indigenous people to Christianity.

A hurricane destroyed the Mission San Antonio de Valero in 1724. The mission then moved to the east bank of the San Antonio River. Construction of the chapel began on May 8, 1744.

In the 1760s, use of the San Antonio mission declined sharply. The mission was finally abandoned in 1793, and it remained empty for the next ten years. Then in 1803, the Second Flying Company of San Carlos de Parras moved into the mission. The company was a group of Spanish soldiers from Alamo de Parras, Coahuila, Mexico. The soldiers used the mission's buildings as barracks for several years.

Historians believe that the mission was renamed the Alamo during this time. Some believe the Alamo was named after the flying company's home city. Others believe the Alamo was named after the cottonwood trees that once grew near the former mission. That's because *álamo* is the Spanish word for "cottonwood."

Mexican forces controlled the Alamo from 1803 to 1835. From 1805 to 1812, the mission served as San Antonio's first hospital. In 1835, Mexican general Martín Perfecto de Cos surrendered the Alamo to Texan forces. This would not be the last time, though, that the Alamo would change hands.

In 1836, the Battle of the Alamo broke out. In the battle, 189 Texans fought for independence from Mexico. They fought against the Mexican army, which had between 1,800 and 5,000 soldiers. The 189 Texans not only lost the Battle of the Alamo, but they all lost their lives. Yet, their defeat became an enduring symbol of courage.

The Battle of the Alamo

DISPUTED LAND

The land on which the Alamo was built has a long history of disputes. The first European explorers in Texas were Spanish. They arrived in the 1500s and claimed the land for Spain. They also claimed neighboring lands, including Mexico.

In the 1600s and 1700s, France tried to seize Texas from the Spanish several times. In 1803, the United States purchased 800,000 square miles (2,000,000 sq km) of land west of the Mississippi. Some of this land bordered Texas, and U.S. and Spanish authorities often disagreed about Texas's borders.

Despite these disputes, Spain allowed U.S. settlers to colonize Texas. One of the most influential men during this time was Moses Austin. Austin was a native of Durham, Connecticut. He wanted to bring Anglo-American settlers to Texas.

Austin arrived in San Antonio on December 23, 1820. He asked the Spanish governor of Texas, Antonio María Martínez, for permission to bring colonists to the area. Martínez turned down Austin's request.

While still in San Antonio, Austin met an old acquaintance, Baron de Bastrop. De Bastrop lived in San Antonio and was impressed with Austin's colonization plan. The two men returned to Governor

In this 1821 mural, Stephen F. Austin and Mexico's land commissioner Baron de Bastrop (seated) issue land to the colonists.

Martínez's office. On December 26, 1820, Martínez approved the plan for colonization. Austin received permission to bring 300 Anglo-American families to Texas.

Moses Austin died on June 10, 1821. On his deathbed, he asked that his son, Stephen F. Austin, continue the colonization effort. In December 1821, Stephen established a colony along the Gulf of Mexico.

The map-making history of Texas is divided into five periods. Stephen Austin drew maps, such as the one on the right, during the third period, which lasted from about 1820 until 1850. Maps made during this period were the first to be based on accurate and detailed surveys, which the settlers required to claim their land. By this period, experienced surveyors used the most modern techniques and instruments available.

CHANGES IN MEXICO

While plans for colonization were underway in Texas, big changes were occurring in Mexico as well. The Mexicans had begun rebelling against Spanish rule in 1810. Battles continued for the next 11 years. Then in 1821, Spanish viceroy to Mexico, Juan de O'Donojú, was forced to sign the Treaty of Córdoba. It established Mexico's independence from Spain.

In 1822, a Mexican revolutionist named Agustín de Iturbide became the emperor of Mexico. He was appointed to that position by his troops. De Iturbide's leadership lasted barely a year before he was forced to flee to Europe. The revolt against Iturbide was led by Antonio López de Santa Anna and Guadalupe Victoria.

Guadalupe Victoria became the first president of Mexico. The Mexican government began to move in a new direction under his leadership. The Constitution of 1824 created the Mexican state of Coahuila y Tejas, or Texas. It also guaranteed Mexican citizens certain rights.

At this time, the Mexican government made land available for Anglo-American settlers. They were invited to make their homes in Texas. During the early 1800s, between 20,000 and 25,000 Americans migrated to Texas. Eventually, there were far more Americans in Texas than there were native Tejano Mexicans.

Opposite page: *Santa Anna*

This new booming population refused to conform to Mexican laws and customs. In response, the Mexican government passed a series of laws in 1830. These laws were designed to slow the immigration process. They were unsuccessful, however, because the Mexican government couldn't enforce them.

A large divide began to grow between the Texans and the Mexicans. The new laws angered the Texans. They were unhappy with the way the Mexican government treated them. Texans also disagreed with the Mexican government's stance against slavery. With so much land to tend and so few people to work it, many Texans believed that they needed slaves to survive financially.

In addition, the Mexican government interfered in what Texans saw as civil matters. These civil matters included trade, legal proceedings, and the master-slave relationship. Meanwhile, the Mexican government couldn't supply timely justice or trials by jury.

In the summer of 1833, Stephen Austin traveled to Mexico City to resolve these issues. He asked Santa Anna, Mexico's new president, to change his government's policies. Santa Anna

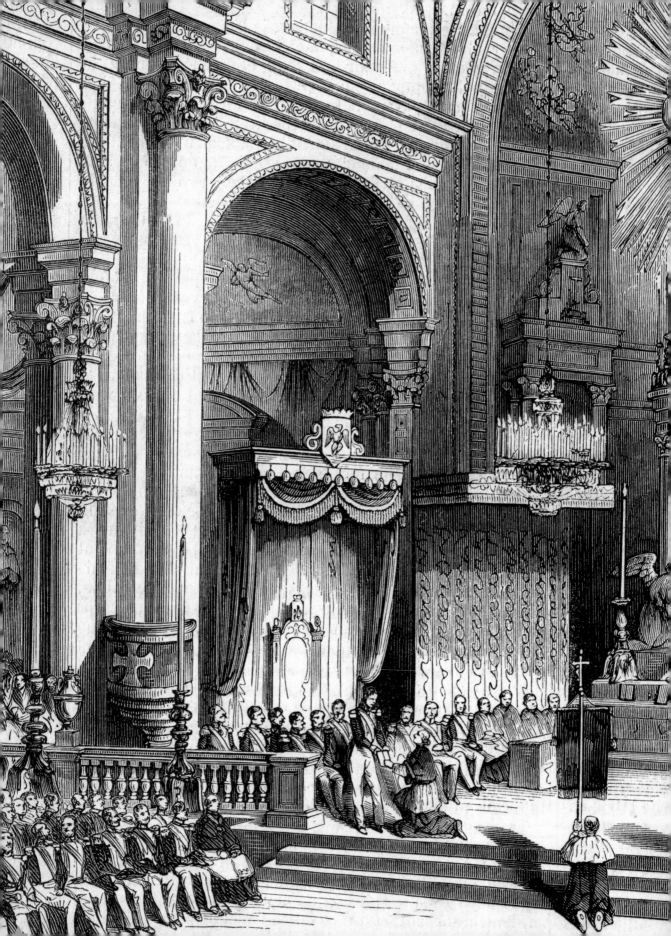

refused Austin's request. Meanwhile, Santa Anna was gaining power throughout the region. He was a military dictator who often violated Mexico's constitution.

In January 1834, Austin was arrested in Saltillo, Mexico. He was suspected of trying to get Texans to oppose the Mexican government. He was returned to Mexico City. Though he was never charged with any crime, Austin remained a prisoner. The Mexican government moved him from one prison to the next until he was finally released in December 1834. The Mexican government kept Austin from returning to Texas until July 1835.

The Texans resented the Mexican government's jailing of Austin. They were also frustrated by the government's ineffectiveness. The Texans' anger reached the boiling point, and an armed conflict was about to take place.

Opposite page: *Inauguration ceremony of Mexican president Santa Anna*

SANTA ANNA

Santa Anna began his military career in 1810 at age 16 as a cadet. For a time, he fought for the Spanish to prevent Mexico's independence. In 1821, he changed sides to help establish Mexican independence. While he was known for his bravery in battle, he was also known for placing his own interests above his country's.

THE BATTLE OF GONZALES

On October 2, 1835, the Mexican government sent 100 Mexican soldiers to Gonzales, Texas. Led by Lieutenant Castaneda, the group's job was to retrieve a cannon that the Mexican government had given to the Texans for protection. Austin led the group of Texan volunteer soldiers who refused to return the cannon.

The confrontation between the Mexican soldiers and the Texans started with words. It then turned physical when the Texans fired a shot from the cannon toward the soldiers. A short battle erupted, leaving one Mexican soldier dead. Lieutenant Castaneda pulled his forces from the area, and they left without the cannon. The Battle of Gonzales marked the first shots of the Texas Revolution.

After the Battle of Gonzales, Texan troops began a siege on the city of San Antonio. On December 5, 1835, Texan military commander Benjamin R. Milam's forces attacked San Antonio. Despite being outnumbered three to one, the Texans prevailed. The Texans had better weapons and superior shooting skills.

Eventually, Mexican general Martín Perfecto de Cos surrendered the city. He and his men were released after they pledged to never again fight the Texans. The city of San Antonio came under Texas control. This included the Alamo, which had been used to house the Mexican military.

Opposite page: *Stephen Austin memorial in Austinville, Virginia, his birthplace*

The colonization of Texas was not Stephen Austin's dream, but his father's, Moses Austin. Yet, after his father's death, Stephen made the dream a reality. He became known as the father of Texas. Stephen died on December 27, 1836, at the age of 43. He was originally buried in Gulf Prairie Cemetery at Peach Point, Brazoria County in Texas. On October 20, 1910, his body was moved to the Texas State Cemetery in Austin, Texas.

THE BATTLE OF THE ALAMO

Tension between Texans and the Mexican government increased. The Alamo became a strategic site in the ongoing struggle. For the Mexicans, it was the first stop on their way into the colonies. For the Texans, the Alamo served as an early frontier lookout post. From this outpost, a soldier could warn fellow Texans of any movement by the approaching enemy.

Concern about the Alamo's safety and its ability to withstand an attack soon arose. On January 14, 1836, Alamo commander James Clinton Neill wrote a letter to General Sam Houston. Neill informed Houston that the soldiers of the Alamo were not prepared to defend themselves against a large enemy attack.

Neill was concerned that he had too few soldiers. He was worried that the threat of the Mexican army was too great. He wrote Houston, "Unless we are reinforced and victualled, we must become an easy prey to the enemy, in case of an attack." Neill was asking for added supplies of food and more men.

Houston understood the threat, but he questioned whether the Alamo was worth protecting. In a letter to Neill, Houston suggested moving all of the Alamo's cannons to the towns of Gonzales or Copano. Houston also recommended that the Texan forces abandon the Alamo and blow it up.

Sam Houston

On January 17, Houston sent Colonel James Bowie and a group of volunteers to San Antonio. When Bowie arrived, he was immediately impressed with the fort. Neill had already decided to defend the Alamo rather than blow it up and retreat. He convinced Bowie that the Alamo was worth defending. It was the only barrier between the Texas settlements and the advancing enemy. On February 2, 1836, Bowie wrote provisional governor Henry Smith that both he and Neill had decided to "die in these ditches" rather than retreat or surrender.

As it turned out, Neill left the Alamo on February 14. He went home to be with his family, some of whom had fallen ill. Neill promised to return within 20 days.

When Neill announced that he would be leaving, the soldiers wondered who would lead them. Some thought that Bowie's experience and fame earned him this position. Instead, Neill chose William Barret Travis as his temporary replacement. Travis was an officer, employed by the army. Bowie was only a volunteer colonel.

Neill's decision caused disagreement among the soldiers. The soldiers had grown used to electing their own officers. They were not used to having officers appointed. The group struck a compromise. Travis would lead the regular soldiers, and James Bowie would be in charge of the volunteers. All orders would require the signature of both men until Neill returned to take over.

On February 23, the Texans learned that Santa Anna's army had reached the Rio Grande. Tension rose inside the Alamo. Travis sent an urgent message to the city of Gonzales, "The enemy in large force is in sight. We want men and provisions. Send them to us. We have 150 men and are determined to defend the garrison to the last." The kind of help they needed would never arrive.

Some who defended the Alamo were Texan militia. They fought alongside military soldiers.

Things grew worse. On February 24, James Bowie fell ill. He was believed to have typhoid pneumonia. William Travis took full command of the forces.

Santa Anna's men were in place. For days, they pounded the Alamo with artillery. On March 1, 1836, only 32 Texas soldiers arrived to help defend the Alamo. They were part of Lieutenant George C. Kimbell's Gonzales Company. The additional soldiers were not nearly enough. In a letter addressed to a friend, Travis wrote of his concerns, "If my countrymen do not rally to my relief, I am determined to perish in the defense of this place, and my bones shall reproach my country for her neglect."

Santa Anna leads his men into battle on horseback.

At 5:00 AM on March 6, 1836, the real battle began. Santa Anna sent his men toward the Alamo from all four directions. The Mexican army was somewhere between 1,800 and 5,000 soldiers strong. The Texan army was believed to have numbered between 189 and 257. Gunfire exploded from all directions.

One of the first men to die was William Travis, leader of the Texan forces. James Bowie, too ill to rise from his cot, was killed in it. The assault on the Alamo lasted no more than 90 minutes. When the battle was over, every Texas soldier was killed. Some died fighting. The others were captured alive and then killed. Historians estimate that nearly 600 Mexicans were also killed or wounded in the battle.

While no adult Anglo-Texan male survived the Alamo, about 20 women and children did. William Travis's slave, Joe, was also spared. The women and children returned to their homes. After the battle, Santa Anna is said to have put survivors Susanna Dickinson and her young daughter, Angelina, on a horse. Susanna's husband, Captain Almeron Dickinson, had just been killed in the Alamo gunfire. Santa Anna told Susanna to deliver a message to Sam Houston. He had her warn Houston that more Texans would die if they didn't stop their revolts.

Opposite page: Texan soldiers make a last stand at the Alamo

✦ THE LAST STAND AT THE ALAMO ✦

The flag that floated over the ill-fated mission fortress The Alamo, at San Antonio, in 1836, was that of the Republic of Texas, then fighting for the right to self-government. Its design was that of the Mexican flag, with the eagle, serpent and cactus replaced by the date 1824. This indicated adherence to the Texas constitution of that date, overthrown by Santa Anna, who established a dictatorship. Besieged by 4,000 troops under Santa Anna, the little garrison of 183 Americans held out 12 days under constant bombardment.

From the flat roof with its thick adobe walls, the Texan sharpshooters directed a devastating fire in the defense described in the diary left by Davy Crockett, famed scout, hunter and Indian fighter whose career ended here. Finally the defenders were so weakened that, after two unsuccessful assaults, an entrance was made through sheer weight of numbers and the five lone survivors were slain. The slogan "Remember the Alamo" became a battle-cry which led to Santa Anna's destruction and the ultimate victory of the Texans.

THE ALAMO FLAG

THE ALAMO'S DEFENDERS

The actions of those who defended the Alamo on March 6, 1836, have been retold throughout history. These men did not protect the fort because they wished to die. Instead, they hoped they would be victorious when reinforcements arrived. They were obedient soldiers, but not suicidal. A few of the men on the Texan side even survived the fighting but were later executed by the Mexicans. But, all the men fighting for independence at the Alamo were killed. Among those who dedicated their lives to protecting the Alamo, were William Barret Travis, James Bowie, and David Crockett.

William Barret Travis was a Texan commander. He was born in South Carolina on August 9, 1809. He grew up in Saluda County, South Carolina. Travis studied law and worked as a lawyer. He married Rosanna Cato at the age of 19. By the time Travis was 20, he and his wife had their first child. They named him Charles Edward Travis.

After his son was born, William Travis held a variety of jobs. He worked as a mason, helped publish a newspaper, and even joined

Colonel Travis offers Texas soldiers the chance to escape before battle, but all remain loyal.

the militia. Travis's life was busy, and his marriage failed. He left his wife, son, and an unborn daughter and headed to Texas. He arrived there in 1831, where he received land from Stephen Austin. Travis planned to work as a lawyer.

Travis joined the Texan forces soon after the conflict broke out between Texas and Mexico. In January 1836, provisional governor Henry Smith assigned Travis to the Alamo. About 30 men were assigned with him.

During the entire 13-day Alamo standoff, Officer Travis was in constant communication with government officials. He was looking for any type of help that might make the effort victorious. Sadly, the new Texas government was unable to assist him. The men of the Alamo paid for this lack of resources with their lives.

Another Texan who became a hero at the Alamo was James Bowie. Bowie was born in Kentucky in 1796. He moved to Louisiana in 1802 and grew up there. In 1828, he moved to Texas. In Texas, Bowie made several Native-American friends as he searched for silver and gold, which were rumored to exist in Texas territory. Bowie later became the leader of the volunteer forces at the Battle of the Alamo.

David, or Davy, Crockett, another well-known hero of the Alamo was born on August 17, 1786, in Greene

James Bowie

Davy Crockett

County, in eastern Tennessee. As a young boy, he worked as part of a cattle drive in 1798. Crockett's boss tried to keep young Davy longer than he'd originally agreed. Davy walked seven miles (11 km) in knee-deep snow to escape. Upon returning home, he worked odd jobs. Crockett married Mary Finley on August 14, 1806. He enlisted in the army as a militia scout in September 1813. The next year, he reenlisted as a third sergeant.

Crockett arrived in San Antonio on February 20, 1836. By this time, he had earned a reputation for his skills as a hunter, sharpshooter, trapper, soldier, and politician. His presence at the Alamo strengthened the courage of the soldiers there.

The Alamo chapel still stands today as a reminder of the heroes who lost their lives for Texas.

REPUBLIC OF TEXAS

On March 1, 1836, just days before the defeat at the Alamo, delegates from Texas, the United States, and Europe met at Washington-on-the-Brazos. This old town is located in present-day Washington County, Texas. The group discussed the liberation of Texas from Mexican control. George C. Childress presented a formal call to free Texas in a resolution he drafted. The next day all the delegates agreed to support Childress's call for Texas's independence. This was the beginning of the Republic of Texas.

The development of the republic was difficult. The heroic defeat at the Alamo was only one of the setbacks for the Texans. On March 13, 1836, the Texan army, at Gonzales, was in full retreat eastward. Though the Texans had won the Battle of Gonzales, the Mexican army had not given up the fight. The Mexicans, under the leadership of Santa Anna, were gaining ground quickly.

On March 17, the Texans crossed the Colorado River. Three days later, they paused to recruit additional reinforcements. Historians estimate that this increased the Texan army to about 1,200 men. General Sam Houston's scouts reported that the Mexican army was some 1,325 strong.

The Mexican army was camped west of the Colorado River. This was not good news for the Texans. More bad news quickly followed.

ANTI-TEXAS MEETING

AT FANEUIL HALL!

Friends of Freedom!

A proposition has been made, and will soon come up for consideration in the United States Senate, to annex Texas to the Union. This territory has been wrested from Mexico by violence and fraud. Such is the character of the leaders in this enterprise that the country has been aptly termed "that valley of rascals." It is large enough to make *nine* or *ten* States as large as Massachusetts. It was, under Mexico, a free territory. The freebooters have made it a slave territory. The design is to annex it, with its load of infamy and oppression, to the Union. The immediate result may be a war with Mexico—the ultimate result *will be* some 18 or 20 more slaveholders in the Senate of the United States, a still larger number in the House of Representatives, and the balance of power in the hands of the South! And if, when in a minority in Congress, slaveholders browbeat the North, demand the passage of gag laws, trample on the Right of Petition, and threaten, in defiance of the General Government, to hang every man, caught at the South, who dares to speak against their "domestic institutions,"what limits shall be set to their intolerant demands and high handed usurpations, when they are in the majority?

All opposed to this scheme, of whatever sect or party, are invited to attend the meeting at the Old Cradle of Liberty, to-morrow, (Thursday Jan. 25,)at 10 o'clock, A. M., at which time addresses are expected from several able speakers.

Bostonians! Friends of Freedom!! Let your voices be heard in loud remonstrance against this scheme, fraught with such ruin to yourselves and such infamy to your country.

January 24, 1838.

As the announcement above demonstrates, not all members of the Union supported the annexation of Texas. Many in the North feared the addition of such a large slave state.

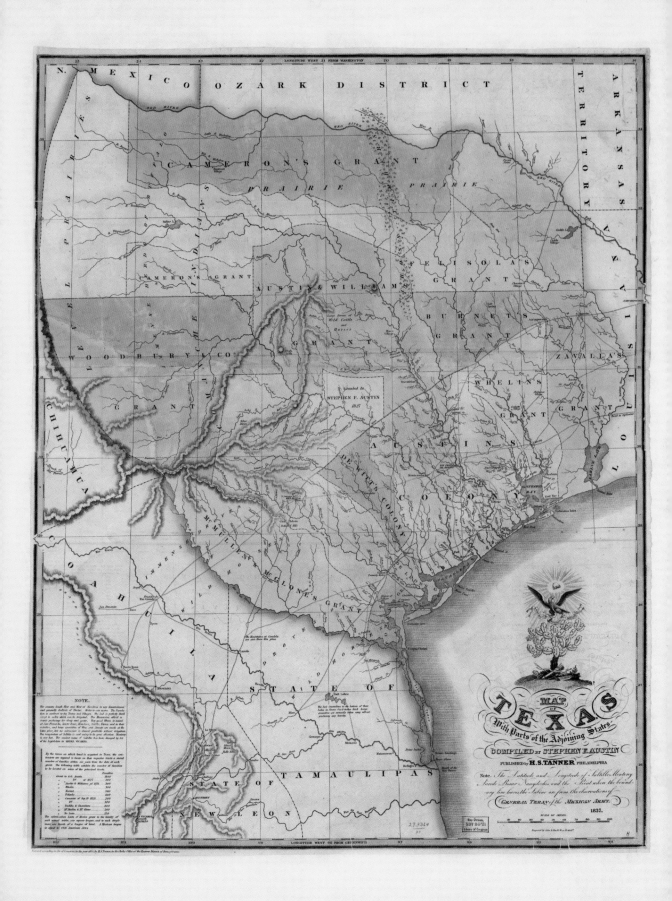

MAP
OF
TEXAS
With Parts of the Adjoining States

COMPILED BY STEPHEN F. AUSTIN

PUBLISHED BY H.S. TANNER PHILADELPHIA

1837

On March 25, Houston's company learned that Texan forces, under the command of Colonel James W. Fannin, were destroyed. These forces had been fighting the Mexican army for control of the city of Goliad.

Throughout the end of March 1836, the Texan army continued to retreat. On March 28, the Texans made their way to San Felipe de Austin. They arrived at the Jared E. Groce plantation two days later. Texas's interim president David G. Burnet ordered Houston to stop his retreat. The Texans had more problems to deal with.

Santa Anna had moved his men toward a new destination. He had decided to take control of the Texas coast and seaports. He crossed the Brazos River on April 11 and arrived in Harrisburg with more than 700 men. He burned the city to the ground and looked to new targets.

Santa Anna was in pursuit of the new Texas government. Members of the government moved from one location to the next, trying to avoid capture by Santa Anna's army. Santa Anna and his army appeared in the town of Morgan's Point on April 19, hoping to capture the government leaders. He believed this would mean the end of the revolution. Much to Santa Anna's disappointment, he found that the government leaders had already left the city. They had moved to Galveston.

News of Santa Anna's movements reached General Houston. He learned that Mexican troops were moving up the west side of the San Jacinto River. The Mexicans had used Vince's Bridge to cross a tributary. Houston knew they would have to use the same bridge to return home.

Opposite page: *An 1837 map of Texas*

Houston seized this opportunity. On April 19, 1836, his soldiers made their way across to the river's west side. The enemy armies, on opposite sides of the San Jacinto River bank, were aware of each other. Both groups had set up their camps. Small fights between the troops led up to something much bigger, the Battle of San Jacinto.

On April 21, Mexican general Martín Perfecto de Cos crossed Vince's Bridge with another 540 troops. Texan spies guessed that the enemy forces now numbered about 1,200 men. General Houston decided that the enemy's reinforcement line had to be cut off.

Houston ordered his troops to destroy Vince's Bridge. This was a risky move for the Texans. With the bridge destroyed, neither the Mexicans nor the Texans could retreat toward the nearby town of Harrisburg. Houston had forced a fight to the finish without knowing who would win.

The Texans destroyed the bridge at nine o'clock the morning of April 21. At 3:30 that afternoon, they attacked. The attack surprised the Mexican forces during their afternoon siesta. As they charged, Texas soldiers cried, "Remember the Alamo! Remember Goliad!" This battle cry was a reminder of the bravery of their fellow Texas patriots.

The battle lasted only 18 minutes. According to Houston's official report, only 9 of the 910 Texans were killed or mortally wounded. The Texas soldiers had killed 630 Mexicans. An additional 730 Mexican soldiers were captured. The Texans also captured large amounts of material goods from the Mexicans. These included muskets, pistols, sabers, mules, horses, clothing, tents, and $12,000 in silver. Unfortunately for the Texans, what they wanted most had escaped them. This was Mexican leader Santa Anna.

CAPTURE OF SANTA ANNA.

*Santa Anna, hiding in tall grass, is captured
a day after the Battle of San Jacinto.*

Santa Anna, who had been at the battle site, had disappeared.
A massive and intense search for the Mexican leader began. The
Texas search party found a man the morning of April 22, 1836.
He was hiding in tall grass, dressed in a Mexican soldier's uniform.
At first, the search team believed that it had merely captured a
runaway Mexican soldier. When the team brought the man back
to its base, the captured Mexican soldiers uttered, *"el presidente."*
Texan soldiers realized the captured man was Santa Anna.

This illustration shows the town of San Jacinto in the late 1800s. Earlier that century, San Jacinto had gained attention because the last battle for Texas's independence was fought there.

Upon learning of the Texan victory in the Battle of San Jacinto, Texas refugee Kate Scurry Terrell described its importance. She said, "As battles go, San Jacinto was but a skirmish; but with what mighty consequences! The lives and the liberty of a few hundred pioneers at stake and an empire won! Look to it, you Texans of today, with happy homes, mid fields of smiling plenty, that the blood of the Alamo, Goliad, and San Jacinto sealed forever Texas, one and indivisible!"

METHODIST CHURCH

JAMES KERR. RES.

DR. Y. D. HARRINGTON. RES.

A. B. McCORMICK RES.

FRANCISCO ESTUDILLO. RES.

J. A. ESTUDILLO. RES.

J. RYAN. RES.

D. McBETH. McCORMICK & WEBER. J. M. LOGSDON. J. RYAN.

FT. STREET

MT. SAN JACINTO.

SKETCHED AND PUBLISHED BY E. S. MOORE.

The Town of **SAN JACINTO** is in Great San Jacinto Valley, Southern R. R. Daily stages meet trains both ways. Propositions for building following advantages and resources: A fertile and varied SOIL, suitable for agric square. WATER in abundance, both mountain and ARTESIAN, seventy-si supply of PINE, CEDAR, OAK and SPRUCE on adjacent mountains, whe HOT MINERAL SPRINGS renowned for curative properties, BATHS F bronchial, asthmatic, catarrhal and rheumatic complaints are benefited and man FIRST-CLASS HOTELS. Settlement began two years ago (1884) and pop ARE CORDIALLY INVITED HERE. For further particulars, address S

..., Cal., twelve miles south of Beaumont (formerly San Gorgonio) on Southern Pacific R. R., and sixteen miles east of Perris, on the California
...Railroad to San Jacinto have been submitted, and its completion within a year is confidently expected. The **SAN JACINTO VALLEY** has the
...raising or grazing, at prices from $15 to $100 per acre. **ORANGES** and all semi-tropical fruits flourish. Amount of tillable lands, twelve miles
...ls at this date (October 1st, 1886). **WOOD** for fuel, $1.00 per cord; two thousand acres heavily timbered land in the valley. An inexhaustible
...ills of 20,000 feet daily capacity. Planing mill, box factory and brickyards running. Brick sold at $6 to $7 per M. Limestone abundant. Two
...Altitude 1,500 feet. **AIR, PURE, DRY** and **LIGHT**, valley sheltered by mountains from high winds, storms and fogs. All pulmonary,
...s permanently cured. A $12,000 **BRICK SCHOOLHOUSE** of four rooms, graded; fine brick **CHURCH**; twenty brick blocks and buildings;
... over one thousand. **ALL INDUSTRIOUS, INTELLIGENT** and **LAW-ABIDING PEOPLE** looking for homes in Southern California,
...CITIZEN'S COMMITTEE, Lock Box 54, San Jacinto, San Diego Co., Cal.

FINAL DEFEAT

The Mexican defeat in the Battle of San Jacinto was the final military event of the Texas Revolution. The Mexican government had little choice now. It had to negotiate with the Texans. The result was the two Treaties of Velasco, which were created on May 14, 1836.

The first treaty is commonly called the Public Treaty of Velasco. This treaty had ten articles and was written in both English and Spanish. The second treaty was referred to as the secret treaty. It stated the terms under which Santa Anna would be released. He would be freed immediately after he agreed to recognize Texas as an independent nation.

While both of these treaties were important, their end results were disappointing. The Texan army refused to free Santa Anna as promised. Meanwhile, the acting Mexican government would not honor promises signed by Santa Anna while he was prisoner. Still, these treaties provided some stable ground. Texans were able to establish a border south of the Rio Grande.

The Texas Revolution had ended, and the newly independent nation needed leadership. On October 22, 1836, Sam Houston became the first regularly elected president of the Republic of Texas. Houston had defeated Stephen F. Austin in the election.

Public Treaty of Velasco

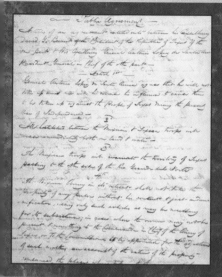

The Treaties of Velasco

Article 1st

General Antonio Lopez de Santa Anna agrees that he will not take up arms, nor will he exercise his influence to cause them to be taken up against the people of Texas, during the present war of Independence.

Article 2nd

All hostilities between the mexican and texian troops will cease immediately both on land and water.

Article 3rd

The mexican troops will evacuate the Territory of Texas, passing to the other side of the Rio Grande del Norte.

Article 4th

The mexican Army in its retreat shall not take the property of any person without his consent and just indemnification, using only such articles as may be necessary for its subsistence, in cases when the owner may not be present, and remitting to the commander of the army of Texas or to the commissioner to be appointed for the adjustment of such matters, an account of the value of the property consumed-- the place taken, and the name of the owner, if it can be ascertained.

Article 5th

That all private property including cattle, horses, negro slaves or indentured persons of whatever denomination, that may have been captured by any portion of the mexican army or may have taken refuge in the said army since commencement of the late invasion, shall be restored to the Commander of the Texian army, or to such other persons as may be appointed by the Government of Texas to receive them.

Article 6th

The troops of both armies will refrain from coming into contact with each other, and to this end the Commander of the army of Texas will be careful not to approach within a shorter distance of the mexican army than five leagues.

Article 7th

The mexican army shall not make any other delay on its march, than which is necessary to take up their hospitals, baggage [---] and to cross the rivers--any delay not necessary to these purposes to be considered an infraction of the agreement.

Article 8th

By express to be immediately dispatched, this agreement shall be sent to General Filisola and to General T.J. Rusk, commander of the texian Army, in order that they may be apprised of its stipulations, and to this they will exchange engagements to comply with the same.

Article 9th

That all texian prisoners now in possession of the mexican Army or its authorities be for with released and furnished with free passports to return to their homes, in consideration of which a corresponding number of Mexican prisoners, rank and file, now in the possession of the Government of Texas shall be immediately released. The remainder of the Mexican prisoners that continue in possession of the Government of Texas to be treated with due humanity -- any extraordinary comforts that may be furnished them to be at the charge of the Government of Mexico.

Article 10th

General Antonio Lopez de Santa Anna will be sent to Veracruz as soon as it shall be deemed proper.

During Houston's first term as president, he faced many challenges. One of these challenges was demilitarizing Texas. This meant that the government let much of the army go. Civilian control took the place of military control. The new government also worked to avoid conflict between the Anglo-American settlers and the Native Americans.

The republic had other problems, too. It was struggling to rebuild itself after the war and had trouble bringing in money. On October 3, 1836, Texas's national debt stood at $1.25 million.

The Texas Congress passed land grants to bring more settlers to the land. Congress hoped that additional settlers would improve the economy. These measures, however, were largely unsuccessful. Money was in such short supply that when Native Americans kidnapped two Texas women and three children, the government lacked the money to hire troops to find them.

Financial woes weighed heavily on the government of Texas. Concerns about border safety troubled them, too. Many leaders began to consider annexation with the United States as a solution to their problems.

Opposite page: *Sam Houston rides into the newly established city of Houston, the first capital of Texas, which was named after him.*

ANNEXATION

In September 1836, Texans voted in favor of becoming citizens of the United States. The request for annexation went to President Martin Van Buren in Washington DC, in August 1837. Van Buren rejected the proposal. He said the United States could not annex Texas because principles in the U.S. Constitution wouldn't allow it. He also believed that annexation might begin a war between Mexico and the United States. Historians believe it was Texas's role as a slave-owning nation that made Van Buren say no.

Great Britain was also against the United States annexing Texas. The British Empire did not want the United States to continue its westward expansion. It was concerned about the trade advantages the United States would gain from the addition of Texas. At one point, the British even considered going to war over the issue.

The British decided against war. Instead, the British government chose to apply political pressure against the annexation of Texas. It convinced the Mexican government to acknowledge the independence of Texas. Mexico would recognize Texas as long as it was not annexed to any country.

Meanwhile John Tyler, who replaced Van Buren as president in 1841, wanted to ensure that Texas did not become part of the British Empire. He drew up a compromise, which promised Texas statehood if it met certain requirements. The U.S. Congress passed Tyler's resolution and urged Texas to accept it.

Texans had a major decision to make as a nation. Texas's president Anson Jones called for a meeting of the Texas Congress on June 16, 1845. In a separate meeting, elected delegates from Texas met on July 4, 1845, to discuss the matter. Both groups had the same choice before them. Texas had to choose annexation by the United States or to be recognized as an independent nation by Mexico.

Both the Texas Congress and the elected delegates voted in favor of annexation. The nation approved the popular vote in October 1845. On December 29, 1845, the U.S. Congress ratified Texas into the Union, making Texas the twenty-eighth state.

President Martin Van Buren

President John Tyler

REMEMBER THE ALAMO

The stand made by the soldiers of the Alamo bought the Texas government more time to establish itself. The government was able to choose independence. It was also able to form a revolutionary government and draft a constitution. Consider what might have happened if Santa Anna had been able to attack the Texas settlements sooner than he did. The Texans would have been less organized and less unified. He could certainly have crushed the rebellion.

A memorial to the soldiers who died in the Battle of the Alamo

The Battle of the Alamo is still honored in Texas. Today, the Alamo is operated by the Daughters of the Republic of Texas (DRT). The DRT is the oldest patriotic women's organization in Texas. It was founded by Betty Ballinger and Hally Bryan in 1891. The two wanted to create a women's organization. They wanted members to be direct descendants of the men and women who helped establish the Republic of Texas.

One of the earliest goals of the group was to convince the Texas government to buy the land of San Jacinto. Another mission was to preserve the memory and voice of the Republic of Texas citizens. This includes all those people who built, fought for, and maintained the freedom of Texas.

In 1905, the DRT became the keeper of the Alamo. This happened due to the efforts of DRT members Clara Driscoll and Adina de Zavala. In an agreement made with the state, the DRT is

The Alamo in San Antonio, Texas

responsible for the upkeep of the Alamo's chapel. It also manages the gardens and surrounding grounds. All of this is done without cost to the Texas taxpayers. The DRT does not charge a fee to visitors.

Today, the Alamo is open to all visitors who are interested in learning about the history of Texas. It stands as a reminder of the brave men who gave their lives to make Texas's independence possible.

TIMELINE

1718   The Alamo, originally known as the Mission San Antonio de Valero, is established.

1793   The mission is abandoned.

1803 to 1835   Mexican forces control the mission. They call it the Alamo.

1821   Moses Austin, who received a land grant to bring Anglo-American settlers to Texas, dies. He asks that his son, Stephen Austin, carry out his mission.

Mexico receives its independence from Spain in the Treaty of Córdoba.

1824   The Constitution of 1824 establishes Mexico as a republic. This constitution guaranteed Mexican citizens certain rights.

1835   The Battle of Gonzales marks the first shots of the Texas Revolution.

1836 The Alamo and the city of San Antonio come under Texas control.

On March 6, every member of the Texas army who fights in the Battle of the Alamo dies.

On April 21, the Texan army defeats the Mexican army in the Battle of San Jacinto.

On April 22, Santa Anna is captured.

The Treaties of Velasco are created on May 14.

Sam Houston becomes the first elected president of the Republic of Texas.

1845 Texas is ratified into the Union on December 29. It becomes the twenty-eighth state.

American Moments

FAST FACTS

While the Alamo was built to serve as a mission it also served as a Mexican army barracks, a hospital, a U.S. Army supply post, and more.

Álamo is the Spanish word for "cottonwood." It is believed that cottonwood trees grew near the group of stone buildings when it was given this name.

Mexico was once Spanish territory.

In the early 1800s, between 20,000 and 25,000 Anglo-Americans migrated to Texas. Eventually, more Americans lived in Texas than did Tejano Mexicans.

Stephen Austin traveled to Mexico City to ask Santa Anna to change his policies regarding Texas citizens. His request was denied, and he was jailed for asking.

In the Battle of the Alamo, historians estimate that the Mexican army was between 1,800 and 5,000 strong compared to the Texan army, made up of 189 soldiers.

Davy Crockett and James Bowie were two of the most famous men to die while defending the Alamo.

When the Texans captured Santa Anna after the Battle of San Jacinto, he was hiding in tall grass, dressed as a Mexican soldier.

The Alamo has been called the shrine of Texas liberty.

WEB SITES
WWW.ABDOPUB.COM

Would you like to learn more about the Battle of the Alamo?
Please visit **www.abdopub.com** to find up-to-date Web site links
about the Battle of the Alamo and other American moments.
These links are routinely monitored and updated to provide the
most current information available.

*This memorial in San Antonio, Texas, pays tribute to
the soldiers who lost their lives at the Battle of the Alamo.*

GLOSSARY

Anglo-American: an American, especially one who lives in the United States, whose language and ancestry is English.

annex: to add land to a nation.

barracks: buildings that house soldiers.

chapel: a place to worship. Usually smaller than or part of a church.

historian: a person who studies and writes about history.

indigenous: native.

interim: the amount of time between two events, or something that happens during an interim period.

militia: an army made up of ordinary citizens.

provisional: for the time being, temporary.

siesta: an afternoon nap taken during the hottest part of the day. Siestas are common in countries with a hot climate, such as Mexico and Spain.

strategic: something that is very important to a plan.

suicidal: intending to end one's life.

Tejano Mexicans: Mexicans who live or lived in Texas.

tributary: a river or stream that flows into a larger stream, river, or lake.

viceroy: the governor of a colony. A viceroy rules on behalf of the country that controls the colony.

No. 3.

Sketch of Texas,

with the Boundaries of Mexican States, as shown
on Genl. Austin's Map of Texas,

Published by H.S. Tanner.
1839.

E. Gilman.
Dr.

Estimated Area.

	in miles	acres.
Texas...	179,567 =	114,082,880

40 106 105 104 102 102 101 100 99 98 97 96 95 94 93 **40 North**

39 39

38 *Arkansas River* 38

37 37

36 36

35 35

34 *NEW MEXICO* *Red River* 34

33 33

32 32

31 *CHIHUAHUA* *Rio Puerco* 31

30 29 28 27 26 27 24 23 22 21 20 19 18 17 16 **30**

29 COAHUILA 29

28 *Rio de la Nueces* 28

27 *Rio Grande or Bravo del Norte* 27

26 R. Salado TAMAULIPAS 26

25 STATE OF 25

24 North NEW LEON

GULF OF MEXICO

INDEX